CW00394455

This Journal

Belongs To:

Printed in Great Britain
by Amazon

60781793R00058